Math Logic Puzzles

Kurt Smith

STERLING PUBLISHING CO., INC.
NEW YORK

This book is dedicated to Cindy Streur
and her sixth-graders at Crestline Elementary
in Vancouver, Washington,
who helped me a great deal
by solving these puzzles, and by telling me
when they were too hard, when they were too easy,
and when they found spelling errors.

Edited by Claire Bazinet

Library of Congress Cataloging-in-Publication Data

Smith, Kurt.
    Math logic puzzles / by Kurt Smith.
        p.   cm.
    Includes index.
    ISBN 0-8069-3864-1
    1. Mathematical recreations. 2. Logic, Symbolic and
mathematical. I. Title.
QA95.S4988   1996
793.7′4—dc20   95-48475
                                                   CIP

10 9 8 7 6 5

Published by Sterling Publishing Company, Inc.
387 Park Avenue South, New York, N.Y. 10016
© 1996 by Kurt Smith
Distributed in Canada by Sterling Publishing
C/o Canadian Manda Group, One Atlantic Avenue, Suite 105
Toronto, Ontario, Canada M6K 3E7
Distributed in Great Britain and Europe by Cassell PLC
Wellington House, 125 Strand, London WC2R 0BB, England
Distributed in Australia by Capricorn Link (Australia) Pty Ltd.
P.O. Box 6651, Baulkham Hills, Business Centre, NSW 2153, Australia
Manufactured in the United States of America
All rights reserved

Sterling ISBN 0-8069-3864-1

CONTENTS

BEGINNING PUZZLES

Fishing

Four men went fishing. They caught six fish altogether. One man caught three, another caught two, one caught one, and one didn't catch anything. Which man caught how many fish? What did each of the fishermen use for bait?

1. The one who caught two fish wasn't Sammy nor the one who used worms.
2. The one who used the flatfish didn't catch as many as Fred.
3. Dry flies were the best lure of the day, catching three fish.
4. Torkel used eggs.
5. Sammy didn't use the flatfish.

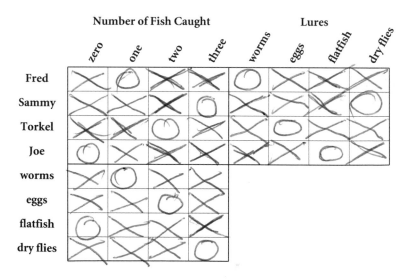

See answers on page 86.

Jump Rope

Some kids were jumping rope (double Dutch) at the school break. They counted how many times each one jumped before missing. See if you can figure out how many jumps each kid made. (You may want to use a pencil and paper to do the adding and subtracting needed to solve this brainer.)

1. Gary jumped eight fewer times than Arnie.
2. Combined, Danielle, and Ruth jumped 37 times.
3. Jan jumped 8 more jumps than Danielle.
4. Gary and Danielle are separated by just three jumps.
5. Arnie's jumps number 5 more than Danielle.

	9	12	17	20	25
Danielle					
Gary					
Jan					
Arnie					
Ruth					

See answers on page 88–89.

Pocket Change

Five boys went to the store to buy some treats. One boy had $4. One boy had $3. Two boys had $2, and one boy had $1.Using the following clues, determine how much money each boy started with and how much each had when he left the store.

The clues are:

1. Alex started with more than Jim.
2. Scott spent 15¢ more than Dan.
3. Duane started with more money than just one other person.
4. Alex spent the most, but he did not end with the least.
5. Dan started with 66% as much as Scott.
6. Jim spent the least and ended with more than Alex or Dan.
7. Duane spent 35¢.

	Started With				Ended With				
	$4	$3	$2	$1	$1.65	95¢	70¢	40¢	10¢
Alex									
Scott									
Dan									
Jim									
Duane									

See answers on page 91.

Temperature

A sixth-grade class project involved keeping track of the average temperature of the classroom over a two-week period in January. The results of the study showed that, at one particular time of the day, the temperature was always at its lowest point. Try to figure out when, during the day, the temperature was lowest, and the reason for it.

1. The automatic heating system in the school comes on at 6:00 in the morning.
2. No students arrive before 8:30. The first temperature reading takes place at that time.
3. The temperature is taken at half hour intervals from 8:30 until 3:00 in the afternoon, when the students go home.
4. The automatic heating system goes off at 2:00.
5. The highest temperature reading is at 10:00.
6. The 2:30 reading of the temperature shows a cooling off, but not the lowest temperature.
7. Morning recess is from 10:20 to 10:35.
8. Afternoon recess takes place from 1:45 until 2:00.
9. The highest temperature over the two-week period was 74 degrees F (23.3 degrees C).

So, when *was* the temperature at its lowest, and why?

See answer on page 93.

EASY PUZZLES

Coast to Coast

Jacques and Chi Chi rode bikes across the United States. They stopped at several major cities along the way. Figure out where they went and the order in which they visited the cities based on the coordinates given in the clues below. (The visited city is the one "closest" to the intersection of the coordinates.)

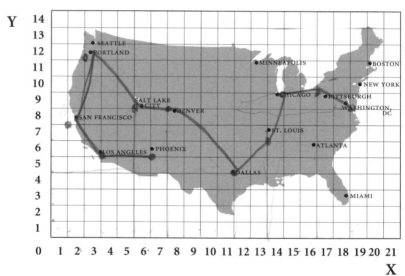

They started their journey at X6,Y5.5.

Their first stop was at X3,Y5.5; then they rode on to X1.5,Y7.5.

Then they stopped off in the city at X2.5,Y11.5.

From there they rode to X5.5, Y8, and then to X7.5,Y8.

They stayed a few days at X11,Y4, and three days at X13,Y6.5.

From there they rode to X13.5, Y9, then to X16.5, Y9.

Finally, tired but happy, they ended their journey at X18, Y8.5.

Start to finish, what are the eleven American cities visited by Jacques and Chi Chi?

See answers on page 85.

Coffee

A few friends meet each morning for coffee. For one of them, it is the only cup of coffee all day. For another, it's only the first of eight cups. Zowie!

Your challenge is to figure out how many cups of coffee each person drinks per day, how many sugar lumps they use per cup, and whether or not they put in milk.

1. Jan uses three times as many lumps as the person who drinks four cups.
2. Three people, including the one who uses four lumps, use no milk.
3. The one who drinks 1 cup a day (not Max) drinks his coffee black without sugar.
4. Doris uses both milk and sugar.
5. Max, who uses no milk, uses half as many sugars as the person who drinks twice as many cups as he does.
6. Boris drinks two more cups than Jan, but Jan uses two more sugars than Boris.

	Cups					Lumps of Sugar					Milk	
	1	4	5	6	8	0	1	2	4	6	Yes	No
Max												
Doris												
Blizzo												
Jan												
Boris												

See answers on page 85.

Decimal Ruler

This ruler measures inches but, instead of measuring them in the usual way, in sixteenths, it measures them in *tenths*. In other words, the standard inch is divided into ten (decimal) units, rather than sixteen units.

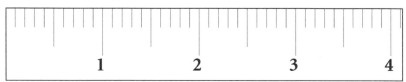

When we measure something with this decimal ruler, it is expressed as the number of inches plus the tenths. For example, the line just below measures 3.4 inches. Go ahead, check it out (mark the length on a straight piece of paper and then hold it next to the ruler).

Now, using paper and this ruler, measure these other lines:

a ⎯⎯⎯⎯⎯⎯⎯⎯⎯⎯⎯⎯⎯⎯⎯⎯⎯

b ⎯⎯⎯⎯⎯⎯

c ⎯⎯⎯⎯⎯⎯⎯⎯⎯⎯⎯⎯⎯⎯⎯⎯⎯⎯

d ⎯⎯⎯⎯⎯⎯⎯⎯⎯⎯⎯⎯

e ⎯⎯⎯

f ⎯⎯⎯⎯⎯⎯⎯⎯⎯⎯⎯⎯⎯⎯⎯⎯⎯

g ⎯⎯⎯⎯⎯⎯⎯⎯⎯⎯

Check your measurements in the solutions.

See answers on page 85.

Destry's Missing Numbers

Destry has five boxes, shown below. Each is supposed to have a decimal number in it, but they're all empty! Help Destry find his missing numbers and put them back in their boxes.

Here are some clues to where the numbers should go:

1. One square (the sum of 11.09, 6.21, and 5.04) is to the left of a square with the difference between 13.27 and 1.34.
2. C is not 13.47 but another square is.
3. One square has a number larger than square B by 13.78.
4. The square with a sum of 13.62, 3.98, 7.00, and .57 is between B and E.
5. The smallest number is B; the largest is E.

left   **right**

   A   **B**   **C**   **D**   **E**

See answers on page 85.

E.F. Bingo

Four girls—Lorraine, Michelle, Wanda, and Sheila—are in a serious game of E.F. Bingo (E.F. stands for equivalent fractions). The first one to fill in a line on her card (up-and-down, across, or diagonally) wins. To solve this puzzle, figure out which girl wins and gets to yell "Bingo!"

The fractions come up and are called in this order:

1. "Four twentieths"
2. "Eighteen twenty-seconds"
3. "Four tenths"
4. "Six tenths"
5. "Two eighths"
6. "Ten sixteenths"
7. "Twelve fourteenths"
8. "Four twenty-eighths"
9. "Six sixteenths"
10. "Six twentieths"
11. "Eight twelfths"
12. "Sixteen eighteenths"
13. "Four twelfths"

E.F. Bingo Cards

¼	⅜	⅛
⁶⁄₇	⅓	²⁄₁₀
⅘	⅗	⁴⁄₁₀

Lorraine

⅖	⅔	⅙
⅐	⅘	⅜
½	³⁄₉	²⁄₆

Michelle

⅝	²⁄₁₀	²⁄₆
⁶⁄₇	⁸⁄₉	³⁄₇
⅓	¼	⁹⁄₁₁

Wanda

½	⅝	³⁄₁₀
¼	⅓	²⁄₁₂
²⁄₆	⁴⁄₁₀	⅔

Sheila

See answer on page 85.

Mountain Climb

Dacon and his friends all went mountain climbing this summer, but not together. They climbed different mountains. Using the clues, see if you can figure out who climbed which mountain, and the heights of the mountains they climbed.

1. Dacon climbed higher than 4500 feet, but not on Goat.
2. Jake climbed higher than both Macom and the one who climbed Sleepy.
3. The mountain which is 9000 feet is not Old Baldy or Goat.
4. The shortest mountain was not climbed by Bacon.
5. Mirre is shorter than the mountain climbed by Macom, but higher than the one climbed by Drakon.
6. Sleepy is not the tallest, but taller than Goat.
7. Raleigh is taller than Goat, which is taller than the ones climbed by Drakon and Dacon.

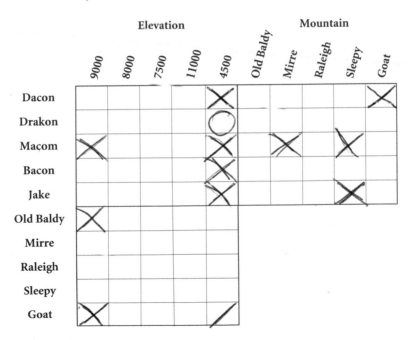

See answers on page 89.

Mountain Race

Five people will race to the tops of mountains of different heights. To have a fair race, each person will carry a weight; the person climbing the lowest mountain, the heaviest backpack weight, etc.

Using the clues, figure out each person's full name, the mountain each will climb, and the weight to be carried in each backpack.

1. Paul's pack weighs 30 lbs.
2. Andy's mountain is 865 ft. higher than the one Brown is climbing.
3. Gerald's pack weighs the same as Dale's minus McGee's.
4. Stiller's pack is half as heavy as the person's climbing Mt. Morgan.
5. Jim's and Dorsey's packs combined weigh 60 lbs.
6. Anderson's pack is 20 pounds lighter than Dale's.

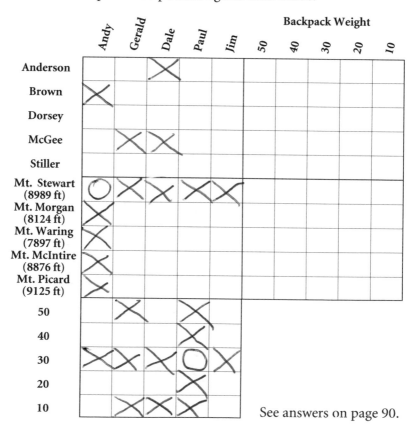

See answers on page 90.

Ned's Newspaper Route

Ned delivers papers in his neighborhood. In January he had 43 customers. He wanted to make a little more money, so he went door to door, and by April he had found five new customers. One new customer gets just a daily paper, two get just a Sunday paper, and two get both. What you need to do is figure out which of his new customers gets what, and the color of their houses (which helps Ned to keep track of things).

1. The Simpsons get both papers; their house is not white.
2. The Browns' house is neither grey nor the color of one of the houses that gets just the Sunday paper.
3. The customer's name who subscribes to just the daily paper begins with J.
4. The customer in the green house does not get a Sunday paper.
5. Mr. Johnson lives in the blue house.

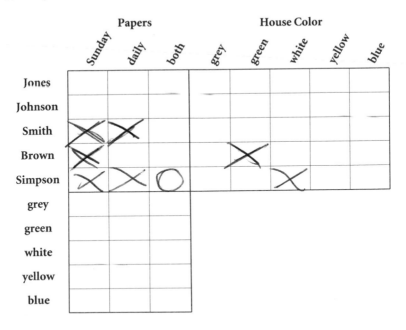

See answers on page 90.

Wild Numbers

A group of untamed, wild numbers has been terrorizing the neighborhood lately. The math police are in need of help rounding them up and placing them in their correct places. Can you help? Will you help? *Please, before it's too late!*

Here are the culprits. They look orderly because they are lined up in three columns, but they really need to be connected up with the correct shapes—six to each shape. Hurry!

.5	100%	75%
⁶⁄₈	³⁄₁₂	⁷⁄₁₄
.75	three-fourths	⁵⁄₂₀
50%	.250	whole
⁴⁄₁₆	$1.00	75¢
⁴⁄₈	⁶⁄₂₄	¹⁰⁄₁₀
one-fourth	half a dollar	³⁄₆
⁵⁄₅	⁹⁄₁₂	⁴⁄₄

¼   ½   ¾   1

See answers on page 94.

Zox

The nation of Zox consists of five islands: Zog, Zod, Zob, Zop, and Zoz. The total population of all five islands is 750 Zoxians.

Figure out how many Zoxians live on each island. Below are some clues to help you.

1. The smallest island has ¹⁄10 as many Zoxians as all of Zox.
2. The largest island is Zod. The smallest island is not Zoz.
3. One island has ⅕ of the total population of Zox. Another island has ⅓.
4. Zob is one and a half times larger than one of the other islands.
5. Zop has 100 more people than the smallest island.

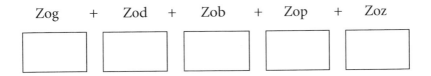

Total population = 750

See answers on page 94.

Hint: Start by figuring out possible populations by using clues 1 and 3.

MEDIUM PUZZLES

Auction

The Clydesdale County Fair held its annual fund-raising auction last week. Five of the people who bought items are listed here.

Your challenge is to match the last names of the purchasers with their first names, identify which items each one bought, and figure out how much each one paid (the lowest amount that anyone paid was $3.50).

Here are a few clues:

1. Elroy is not Grey.
2. The man who bought the coffee paid the highest price, twice that of the fruit.
3. The cheese sold for $2.00 less than the coffee and was purchased by Black.
4. Ms. Green bought the pie for ⅔ the cost of the cake.
5. White and Duane shared their cake and coffee.
6. The pie cost $0.50 more than the fruit.
7. Dan paid $6.00 for his item.
8. Neither Elroy, Denise, nor Black paid over $5.00.

See answers on page 84.

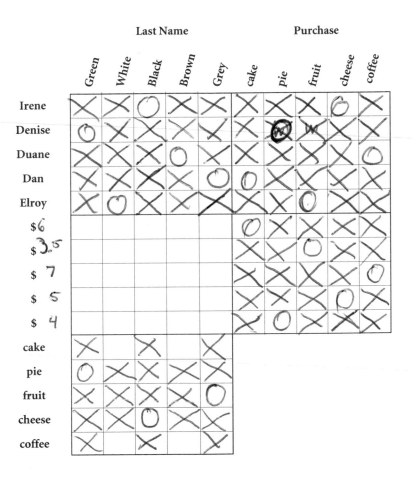

Last Name | Purchase

	Green	White	Black	Brown	Grey	cake	pie	fruit	cheese	coffee
Irene	X	X	O	X	X	X	X	X	O	X
Denise	O	X	X	X	X	X	⊗	W	X	X
Duane	X	X	X	O	X	X	X	X	X	O
Dan	X	X	X	X	O	O	X	X	X	X
Elroy	X	O	X	X	X	X	X	O	X	X
$6						O	X	X	X	X
$3.5						X	X	O	X	X
$7						X	X	X	X	O
$5						X	X	O	X	X
$4						X	O	X	X	X
cake	X		X		X					
pie	O	X	X	X	X					
fruit	X	X	X	X	O					
cheese	X	X	O	X	X					
coffee	X		X		X					

Hint: Start by working out the prices as early as possible.

23

Biology Class

Kristi and five of her friends have each adopted an animal in the biology class at their high school. Using the clues listed below, see if you can figure out which animal (the W's) belongs to which student (the K's).

1. Walter can fly; Willy can't.
2. Kristi's animal is 14 cm (6 in) long.
3. The ladybug is not a lady, nor the smallest.
4. Willy is 5 cm (2 in) shorter than the largest animal.
5. Kyle's animal is neither a fly nor a ladybug.
6. Walter is 10 cm (4 in) shorter than the bat, who's 3 cm (about 1 in) shorter than Wendy.
7. Wanda is the largest.
8. Kurt's animal is the smallest.
9. The hamster belongs to Kevin.
10. Willy is neither the rat nor the hamster.
11. Weldon, who is able to fly, belongs to Kristen.
12. Kate's adoption measures 18 cm (7 in).

See answers on page 84.

	Animal						Name						Measurement					
	bat	hamster	mole	rat	fly	ladybug	Willy	Wendy	Wanda	Walter	Weldon	Warren	1 cm	1.3 cm	11 cm	14 cm	18 cm	23 cm
Kate	X	O	X	X	X	X	O	X	X	X	X	X	X	X	X	X	O	O
Kristen	X	X	⊗	X	X	O	X	X	X	O	X	X	X	O	X	X	X	X
Kurt	X	X	X	X	O	X	X	X	X	O	X	X	O	X	X	X	X	X
Kristi	X	X	X	O	X	X	X	O	X	X	X	X	X	X	X	O	O	X
Kyle	O	X	X	X	X	X	X	X	X	X	O	X	X	X	O	X	X	X
Kevin	X	O	X	X	X	X	X	X	O	X	X	X	X	X	X	X	X	O
1 cm	X	X	X	X	O	X	X	X	X	O	X							
1.3 cm	X	X	X	X	X	O	X	X	X	O	X							
11 cm	O	X	X	X	X	X	X	X	O	X								
14 cm	X	O	X	X	X	X	O	X	X	X								
18 cm	X	X	O	X	X	X	O	X	X	X								
23 cm	X	X	X	O	X	X	X	O	X	X								
Willy	X	X	O	X	X													
Wendy	X	X	X	O	X													
Wanda	O	X	X	X	X													
Walter	X	X	X	O	X													
Weldon	X	X	X	X	O													
Warren	X	X	X	X	X													

Caleb's Checkbook

Five people were discussing their checking accounts. Caleb, who is a spendthrift, is almost broke. But Ms. Wilson still has good bit of her earnings left. Can you figure out how much money each of the five people start with in their checking accounts, what their current balances are, and what are their full names?

Here are a few clues:

1. Joyce is not Jones.
2. Caleb's bills amounted to $1919.00 for the month.
3. Millard, who started with more than Jackson or Brown, ended with less than either Caleb or Wilson.
4. Joyce's balance was exactly half of what she started with.
5. Sam's and Jackson's balances, when added together, were $1427.00.
6. Millard's bills were: rent $850.00, telephone $95.00, utilities $220.00, insurance $400.00, car payment $290.00, food $240.00.
7. Brown spent the least amount on bills — $695.00. Smith spent the most.
8. Barbara's bills totaled $1326.00.

So, who is who and how much money did they each start out and end up with?

See answers on page 84.

	Last Names					$ Started With					$ Ended With				
	Brown	Jones	Smith	Wilson	Jackson	2050	1987	1940	1749	1699	1004	970	423	68	-45
Caleb															
Barbara															
Sam															
Joyce															
Millard															
1004															
970															
423															
68															
-45															
2050															
1987															
1940															
1749															
1699															

Chicken Mountain

At the top of Chicken Mountain live five chicken farmers. Each farmer thinks his chickens are the best. Farmer McSanders says his chickens are best because they lay the most eggs. Farmer Saffola says his chickens make the best fryers.

See if you can figure out which farmer does have the best chickens, based on the following facts plus the formula provided to grade the chickens.

1. The chickens with the best feathers live on the McCombe farm. They sell for $0.73.
2. The chickens which sell for $0.64 produce 105 eggs per day. It's not the Poularde farm.
3. Farmer Saffola has 500 chickens.
4. The farm which produces 115 eggs per day sells its chickens for $0.71.
5. The smartest chickens live on the McPlume farm.
6. The best fryers get the most money.
7. Farmers McSanders and McPlume have 833 chickens between them.
8. The smallest farm produces the most eggs and the second-best price.
9. The biggest chickens produce 4.8 eggs per chicken on the Poularde farm.

See answers on page 84.

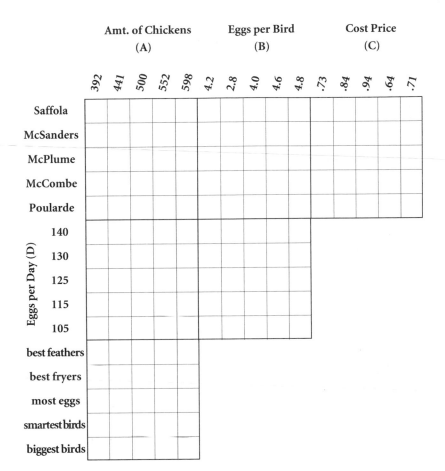

**Best Chickens on
Chicken Mountain
Grading Formula:**

$A \div B \times C + D$

Chocolate Chip Cookies

Five of the world's foremost chocolate chip cookie bakers arrived for the annual Cookie Fiesta. While the bakers all agreed on most of the ingredients that go into their famous chocolate chip cookies, they did not agree at all on the right number of chips per cookie or the amount of time they should be baked to come out perfect. Determine the full names of the five cookie bakers, the number of chips each puts in her cookies, and how long they leave them to bake.

Here are a few clues:

1. Ms. Strudel bakes her cookies for 17 minutes 7 seconds.
2. Effie uses 2 chips fewer than Ruby does.
3. Ms. Applestreet bakes her cookies 51 seconds longer than Thelma does.
4. Ms. Spicer uses one less chip than Ms. Applestreet puts in her cookies.
5. Ms. Honeydew uses more chips than Ms. Spicer does.
6. Ruby isn't Ms. Honeydew.
7. Ms. Spicer bakes for less time than do either Miriam or Georgia.
8. The woman who bakes her cookies for 17 minutes 7 seconds uses 7 chips.
9. Georgia bakes hers for 17 minutes 8 seconds, 1 second longer than Ruby does.
10. The person using 5 chips isn't Ms. Spicer.

See answers on page 84.

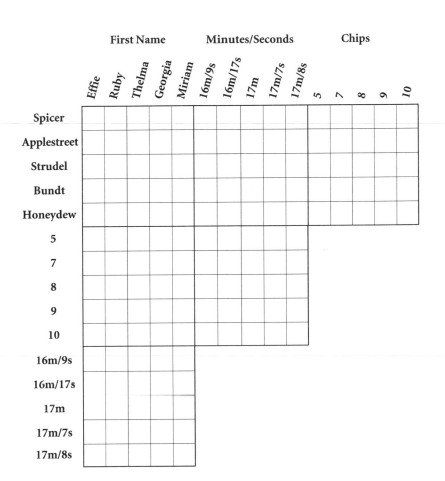

	First Name					Minutes/Seconds					Chips				
	Effie	Ruby	Thelma	Georgia	Miriam	16m/9s	16m/17s	17m	17m/7s	17m/8s	5	7	8	9	10
Spicer															
Applestreet															
Strudel															
Bundt															
Honeydew															
5											
7											
8											
9											
10											
16m/9s						
16m/17s						
17m						
17m/7s						
17m/8s						

Hint: Clues 4, 5, and 10 are the key ones.

Dessert

Four friends went out to a new restaurant to try their desserts. Although some were very hungry, others weren't so they didn't eat the full portions they were served.

Using the clues, determine the full names of the four friends, the kind of dessert each had, and the amount eaten.

1. Ms. Jones' dessert had been cut into eight pieces.
2. Jane ate her dessert with a spoon. It was served in a measuring cup that was divided into three equal-size portions. She ate the dessert down to the bottom line.
3. The one who ate the fig cookie was neither Smith nor Jane.
4. The apple pie was cut into six pieces.
5. Pete and Grey play basketball together.
6. Brown and Tom paid for the meal.
7. Pete's dessert wasn't divided into thirds.
8. Grey didn't eat any dessert beginning with the letter C.
9. The fig cookie was sliced into quarters. The person who ate it left one of the pieces.
10. The apple pie wasn't eaten by Grey or Sarah.
11. No one has a first and last name that begin with the same letter.

See answers on page 85.

	Last Name				Portion Eaten				Dessert			
	Smith	Brown	Grey	Jones	⅙	¾	⅔	⅛	fig cookie	apple pie	custard	choc cake
Jane												
Pete												
Tom												
Sarah												
fig cookie												
apple pie												
custard												
choc cake												
⅙												
¾												
⅔												
⅛												

Dog Apartments

Six dogs live in the Airedale Apartments. Each dog lives on a different floor, eats a different amount of dog food (in pounds) each week, and takes a different number of baths each month. Using the clues below, figure out which floor each dog lives on, the amount of food each one eats, and the number of baths each one takes. Watch out for tricks!

1. The dog in 221 eats twice as much as the one who takes 1 bath a week.
2. MacTavish eats four pounds less than Spunky, but takes five more baths.
3. The dog that eats 32 pounds a month takes 3 baths a week.
4. Wilfred lives two floors above Spunky. Spunky lives two floors above Chico.
5. Taz and the dog on the 6th floor eat a combined weight of 80 pounds in a month.
6. The dog in 341 eats 24 pounds a month and bathes once a week.
7. The dog in 408 eats fewer pounds in a month than he takes baths.
8. The dog on the 5th floor eats 16 pounds a month and takes one less bath than Chico.

See answers on page 85.

	Apartment No.						Food per Week						Baths per Month					
	103	*221*	*341*	*408*	*512*	*609*	*2*	*4*	*6*	*8*	*10*	*12*	*2*	*3*	*4*	*6*	*9*	*12*
MacTavish																		
Chico																			
Ivan																			
Wilfred																			
Taz																			
Spunky																			

Baths

	103	*221*	*341*	*408*	*512*	*609*	*2*	*4*	*6*	*8*	*10*	*12*
2												
3												
4												
6												
9												
12												

Food

	103	*221*	*341*	*408*	*512*	*609*
2						
4						
6						
8						
10						
12						

Field Trip

Duloc and his pals held bake sales and earned enough money to take a field trip with their teacher, Mr. Oonla. In fact, they made enough to go all the way to the planet Earth!

When they arrived at the third planet in the Sol system, they discovered the gravitational pull was very different from what they were used to back on Nolu Si. Mr. Oonla was curious about the difference in weight, how much his students weighed in Earth ounces. An Earth ounce is equivalent to 11 Nolu Si ounces, except that on Nolu Si the measurement isn't called ounces but qinae.

According to the following clues, how much in Earth ounces do each of these five students weigh? How much do they weigh back on Nolu Si?

1. Sio weighs 50.6 qinae. He outweighs everyone except Phren, who weighs 13.2 qinae more.
2. Ontrus, the lightest, weighs 27.5 qinae less than Duloc.
3. Jorn weighs 5.5 qinae less than Sio, and 2.2 qinae more than Duloc.

	ounces	qinae
Jorn		
Duloc		
Phren		
Sio		
Ontrus		

See answers on page 86.

Hint: Phren is a bit chubby. Ontrus is a little skinny.

Flea Market Leftovers

There were a few unsold items, listed below, left over from the flea market. Bernie told some friends who had helped her with the sale to each take one of the items home. Can you figure out who took which item?

Item	Measurement
Nut	diameter 1.25 in
Pencil	end to end 17.2 cm
Compass	height 16.5 cm
Pencil sharpener	height 5½ in
Bolt	length 4.5 cm

Note: Whether in inches or in centimetres, each item is measured in only one direction.

1. Dan took one item which was shorter than the item Sandy took by 1.3 centimetres.
2. The item taken by Bob was one and one-quarter inches taller than the item taken by Irene.
3. Doris's item was 7 centimetres less than Bob's.
4. Sandy's item was 12 centimetres less than Doris's.

See answers on page 86.

Four Cups

A   B   C   D

Four cups, A to D, are arranged side by side. Each contains a certain amount of liquid measured in ounces. One cup contains water, another oil, one holds vinegar, and the other apple juice. Which cup has which liquid and how much is in each?

Here are some clues:

1. The cup with oil is between the cups containing 3 oz. and 5 oz.
2. The vinegar isn't in cup C.
3. There's more apple juice in the cups than water, but more oil than apple juice.
4. The water is between the juice and the oil.
5. The difference in ounces between the vinegar and the juice is 3.
6. Cup D doesn't contain oil, and doesn't have the least amount of liquid in it.
7. Cup C has more liquid than does cup A.
8. The cup with 11 oz. isn't vinegar.

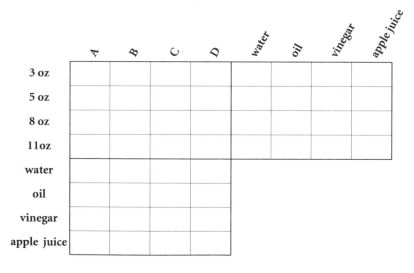

See answers on page 87.

Fractions Prom

The annual Fractions Prom was held last week. Six couples went to the dance together. They sat at three tables. Because One Third and Three Fifths were still angry at each other over an argument about which of them was more important, they refused to sit together. Otherwise, everybody got along quite well.

From the following clues, see if you can figure out which fractions went to the prom with which other fractions, and which of the three tables they shared.

1. One Eighth and his date shared a table with One Fourth and her date, but it was not table 3.
2. The sum of One Tenth and her date was ½. The sum of everyone at that table was 1 ³⁄₁₀.
3. One Sixth and Three Eighths didn't share a table.
4. One Third and his date totaled 1.
5. Seven Eighths and Three Eighths shared table 2. Their dates totaled ⅜.
6. One Fifth's date is not Two Thirds.

	Two Thirds	One Sixth	Three Fifths	One Fourth	Three Eighths	One Tenth
One Third						
Five Sixths						
One Eighth						
One Fifth						
Seven Eighths						
Two Fifths						

Table 1	Table 2	Table 3

See answers on page 87.

Fund-Raiser

Three eighth-grade classes at a large school competed in a fund-raising event by reading books. The person who read the most books won a CD player. The class that read the most books won a field trip to an amusement park. No two students read the same number of books.

From the following clues, which student won the player, and which class got to go to the amusement park?

1. Sam, in room 125, read half as many books as Eric, who read half as many as Danny.
2. Nancy read twice as many books as Harry, who is in room 125.
3. Room 125 includes the students who read 24 books and 34 books.
4. Teresa read three times as many as Sam.
5. Bill is in room 208, which totaled 113 books.
6. Jennifer read half as many books as Tinzen.
7. There are just three students in room 214, including Jennifer, Jerry, and the winning student.
8. Dennis read ten more books than Nancy.
9. Bill read just one more book than Harry.
10. No one in room 214 read fewer than 21 books.
11. The winning room included the person who read the fewest books.
12. The total number of books read in room 214 was 91.
13. Joan read fewer books than Julia, who read more books than Jerry.

	Books Read													**Rooms**		
	9	12	13	18	21	23	24	27	28	32	34	36	42	125	208	214
Nancy																
Bill																
Jerry																
Sam																
Tinzen																
Julia																
Harry																
Eric																
Jennifer																
Teresa																
Danny																
Joan																
Dennis																

See answers on page 87.

Golf

Four friends played golf. The scorekeeper wasn't alert and missed recording a few scores. Find the correct missing scores and figure out everyone's total. All four players had different scores.

Oh yes, and who was the lazy scorekeeper?

Hole	1	2	3	4	5	6	7	8	9	Total
Par	4	5	3	4	4	5	4	4	3	36
Jim	5	5	4	4	6		5	3		
Jan		7	3	4	5	5	5		3	
Jon	6	5	4	5	5		4	5		
Jed	5	6		4	5	6		6	4	

1. Jan had the lowest scores on holes #1 and #6.
2. The total scored for hole #3 was 14.
3. Jed's total score was higher than Jan's.
4. The total score for all four players was 169.
5. Just one player shot a birdie (1 under par)— Jim, 3 on #8.
6. The scorekeeper's total score was 44—the highest.
7. Jon shot par on one of his missing scores. He shot one over par on the other.
8. The total scored for hole #6 was 23.
9. Jim's total score was higher than Jan's, but not as high as Jon's.

See answers on page 87.

Grade Book

A math teacher gives a test once a week. All the students took all the tests. Unfortunately, the teacher forgot to record some of the scores. Find each student's missing test score, then total their scores and find the students' averages and final grades.

Average	Grade
62–70	A
57–61	B
52–56	C
49–51	D

Test	1	2	3	4	5	6	7	8	9
Alban	45	56	84	36	78	34	46		98
Astrid	49	60		50	86	45	36	20	87
Amos	38	70	90		100	48	38	20	97
Angus	39		94	50	94	49	45	19	100
Avril	44	68	88	50	89		39	20	100

1. Astrid's missing test score is the same as the average of the student with the A.
2. Amos got a perfect score on test 2. Angus missed it by 2 points.
3. The total of all five students' total scores is 2628.
4. The missing score on test 8 is 18. On test 6 it's 33.

See answers on page 87.

Hint: Start with clue 2.

Hot Dogs

One student from each fifth-grade class in McDonald Elementary School decided to try to set a new school record for the most hot dogs eaten during one lunch period.

From the following clues, see if you can tell how many hot dogs each student ate, the students' last names, and their room numbers. (Two hot dog eaters are still sick at home!)

1. Isabella, whose last name is not Green, ate three-fourths as many hot dogs as Tony.
2. Ginger is in room 203.
3. Brown ate four more hot dogs than Gerald, and two more than White.
4. Green's room is between Gerald's and Ginger's rooms.
5. Germaine ate more hot dogs than Gerald, who ate more than Green.
6. The student from room 204 ate 8 fewer hot dogs than the student in room 201
7. Smith's classroom is 202.

See answers on page 88.

Hot Dogs Eaten Rooms

	Smith	Jones	Green	Brown	White	12	16	20	22	24	201	202	203	204	205
Gerald															
Isabella															
Germaine															
Tony															
Ginger															
201															
202															
203															
204															
205															
12															
16															
20															
22															
24															

Hint: Work on figuring out the rooms first.

Longest Drive

Six golfers thought they were pretty "hot off the tee," so they had a contest to see who could hit the ball farthest. The golfers used four different-size clubs.

When they tried to compare the distances, they discovered that some had been measured in yards and some in metres. Confusing? Not if you are good at converting metres to yards, or vice versa.

From the clues below, determine who the golfers are, how many yards or metres each one hit the ball (rounded off to whole numbers), and the club size each one used. (If needed, refer to the simple yards/metres conversion formulas at the bottom of this page.)

1. Henry did not use his driver when he hit his booming 282-metre drive. Two of the guys did, including Baring.
2. The longest drive was hit with a driver, but not by Reed or Simon.
3. The shortest drive, 244 metres, was hit with a 5-wood, but not by Bates or Jake.
4. Desmond's drive went 257 metres, 4 yards shorter than Pym's.
5. The 2-iron drive went 263 metres, 20 fewer than Lester's.
6. Lyle used the 5-wood.
7. Henry and Rivers each used their 3-woods. Henry's went 23 yards farther.

See answers on page 89.

Conversion Formulas:
  Metres × .92 = yards
  Yards × 1.09 = metres

	Baring	Bates	Jenkins	Pym	Reed	Rivers	3-wood	2-iron	driver	5-wood
Desmond										
Simon										
Lyle										
Lester										
Henry										
Jake										
257m										
283m										
263m										
244m										
261m										
282m										
3-wood										
2-iron										
driver										
5-wood										

Lunch at Paul's

Paul invited some friends for lunch and asked each to bring two items. Everyone already had one item and they brought that, but they had to buy a second item at the store. Using the clues and the price list below, figure out who brought which items, and how much each person spent—including Paul, who bought the coffee.

Purchased Items	Price List
chicken	$6.40 pound
coffee	$5.50 pound
cheese	$4.80 pound
mayonnaise	$1.09 per 8-oz jar
bread	$1.39 loaf

1. Julie bought 9 ounces of one of her items, which cost her $2.70. She did not bring fruit.
2. The person who brought the salad also bought three loaves of bread.
3. Sandra bought two 8-ounce jars of mayonnaise but did not bring the fruit or the cake.
4. Paul needed pickles and salad. Wally brought one of them.
5. Diane's purchase was 12 ounces and it cost her $4.80.
6. The person who paid $2.75 for half a pound also brought the olives.

See answers on page 89.

	Brought					Bought					Cost				
	pickles	salad	cake	olives	fruit	coffee	bread	cheese	mayo	chicken	$2.18	$2.75	$4.80	$2.70	$4.17
Paul															
Julie															
Sandra															
Diane															
Wally															
$2.18															
$2.75															
$4.80															
$2.70															
$4.17															
coffee															
bread															
cheese															
mayo															
chicken															

Multiplication Jeopardy

For a change, Dale and some friends studying for a multiplication test gave each other the problem answers (products) and tried to figure out the two numbers in the problem. From the clues, figure out each student's full name, the product each was given, and the correct multiplier and multiplicand. One of the products (where multiplicand and multiplier intersect) is 144.

1. Dale's multiplicand is 14.
2. Tina's last name is not Johns.
3. June's multiplier is 9.
4. Neil is neither James nor Jones.
5. Miss Jensen's product is 120.
6. The person whose multiplicand is 13 is not James, Jensen, or Mr. Johnson.
7. Tina's product is 143.
8. Neil's multiplicand is 18. His product is 126.
9. Johns's multiplier is 7.

Multiplicand

	Sue	June	Dale	Neil	Tina	13	14	15	16	18
James										
Jones										
Jensen										
Johns										
Johnson										
5										
7										
8										
9										
11										

Multiplier (for rows 5, 7, 8, 9, 11)

See answers on page 90.

Old House

Six different families have lived a total of 88 years in an old house. The original owners lived there half the total number of years. A second family lived there a quarter of the years. The third family lived in the house half that. Then a family lived there five years. The fifth family lived there two years. And the sixth family still lives there.

Each family painted the house a different color. Right now, it is white. How long did each family live in the old house? What color did each family paint it?

1. The Smiths lived there eleven times longer than the Parkers.
2. The house was yellow for two years.
3. In all, the house was painted three different colors—blue, yellow, and white—for 11 years.
4. The color was changed from green to brown after the Carpenters moved.
5. The house was either brown or red for 33 years.
6. The Barneses lived there longer than the number of years the house was blue and white.
7. The house was yellow when the Warners moved in.

	Barnes	Carpenter	Lewis	Parker	Smith	Warner	blue	brown	green	yellow	white	red
no. years												
blue												
brown												
green												
yellow												
white												
red												

See answers on page 90.

Play Ball

Toddy and some of her friends in a writing class had to bring a ball, representing their favorite sport, to class along with a composition that they had written about the sport. Toddy brought the ball weighing the least.

From the clues below, figure out who brought which ball, how much each ball weighed (in ounces), and what color it was.

1. The golf ball weighed less than the ball that Tanya brought, and also less than the brown ball.
2. Tom's ball weighed more than the red one.
3. The soccer ball, which was 14.5 ounces heavier than Teresa's ball, was not orange.
4. The person who brought the orange ball was not Teddie, whose ball weighed 15.2 ounces more than the Ping-Pong ball.
5. The ball that weighed more than all of them except for one was white.
6. The heaviest ball was the basketball, and the lightest one was yellow.
7. The 2-ounce ball was green, and smaller than the red one and the ball brought by Teddie.
8. The ball brought by Tillie was ten times heavier than the golf ball.

See answers on page 91.

	orange	white	green	red	brown	yellow	1.5	.8	15	22	2	16
Teddie												
Teresa												
Toddy												
Tanya												
Tom												
Tillie												
Ping-Pong												
tennis												
golf												
soccer												
basketball												
football												
1.5												
.8												
15												
22												
2												
16												

Potato Chips

Everyone in Mr. Glitzwhizzle's classroom agreed that no one could eat just one potato chip, but decided to have a contest to see who could eat the most in three minutes. Five students, and Mr. Glitzwhizzle himself, entered the race. From the clues below, figure out the last names of the students and Mr. Glitzwhizzle's first name, and how many bags of chips (the small size) each one ate.

1. Witteyspooner and Gazelda together didn't eat as many bags as Elmo or Jones did.
2. Hubert ate twice as many bags as Grugenminer.
3. Sally's last name does not start with G.
4. Kettledrummel ate one-fourth as many bags as Hubert did.
5. Mr. Glitzwhizzle ate 18 bags. Gerald could eat only half that many.
6. Hubert ate as many bags as Elmo and Gazelda combined.

	Glitzwhizzle	Kettledrummel	Grugenminer	Crackenberry	Witteyspooner	Jones	3	6	9	12	18	24
Gazelda												
Gerald												
Hubert												
Sally												
Amos												
Elmo												
3						
6						
9						
12						
18						
24						

Bags

See answers on page 91.

Queen Rachel's Bridge Toll

When the new Queen Rachel Bridge was built across the Queen Rachel River, Queen Rachel decided to charge a toll. Each person who crosses the bridge is charged .05 of the value of their shoes! So, if a person's shoes are worth $1.00, that person has to pay 5¢ in toll. With the information below, figure out how much each person has to pay to cross the Queen's bridge, and the color of their shoes.

1. Kurt's shoes are not green, nor is green the color of the shoes worth $3.60.
2. The person with the blue shoes must pay 36¢ toll.
3. Taber pays a higher toll than Cindy. Neither of them wears black shoes.
4. The person whose shoes are worth $3.60 is not Caleb.
5. One person, whose shoes are not green or red, pays an 18¢ toll.
6. The person with the red shoes pays 14¢ toll.
7. Caleb pays 24¢.
8. The person with the white shoes pays 38¢ toll.
9. Cindy's shoes are blue.

| | Value of Shoes | | | | | Shoe Color | | | | |
	$2.80	$3.60	$4.80	$7.20	$7.60	red	green	blue	white	black
Chiquita										
Cindy										
Kurt										
Taber										
Caleb										
red										
green										
blue										
white										
black										

See answers on page 91.

Rhoda Tiller

Someone has given these five figures actual names! Can you believe it? Using your protractor, measure the angles below, then use the clues, giving interior or exterior angles, to figure out who is who.

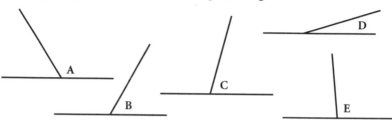

1. Ms. Veda measures 105 on the outside.
2. Mr. Able's exterior angle is 122.
3. The 61-angle figure is not Asper or Rhoda.
4. Tiller has the 163 outside measurement.
5. The figure with the 95 angle is not Ed, Val, or Ruta.
6. Gus's interior angle is 85. Baggy's is not 58.
7. Rhoda's outside angle measures 163.
8. Neither Mr. Able nor Ruta is the 75er.

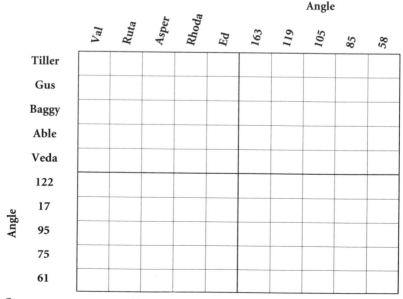

See answers on page 91.

Sand

Six men divided 120 pounds of sand to be used for concrete projects they were building. Mr. Thomas's project was a good bit smaller than Mr. Logan's project, so Mr. Thomas needed less sand.

The pie chart below shows the distribution of the sand among the six men. Using the chart, clues provided, and your ability to convert the percentages into weight in pounds, figure out how much sand each man took.

1. Mr. Logan took just a little over 26 pounds, which was not the most taken.
2. Mr. Driver took the least amount.
3. Mr. Antonelli took 30 fewer pounds than Mr. Lang.
4. Mr. Waters took twice as much sand as Mr. Driver and Mr. Thomas combined.

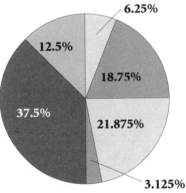

Builder	Sand Taken %	Pounds
Mr. Logan		
Mr. Driver		
Mr. Thomas		
Mr. Lang		
Mr. Antonelli		
Mr. Waters		
Total Sand	100%	120

See answers on page 92.

Shapes

The shapes on this page are measured in decimal units. Your job is to create a new shape (which will not be a square or a rectangle) using the lines described in the clues. Your shape must show the decimal units, just as mine do.

1. The top line of your shape is half as long as the combined distance of the top of B and the side of C.
2. The bottom line of your shape is the same length as the top of C less the top of A multiplied by 1.5.
3. The left side of your shape is twice as long as two sides of B less one side of C. This side is perpendicular to the top line.
4. The right side of your shape is the same length as the top of C less one half the top of A.

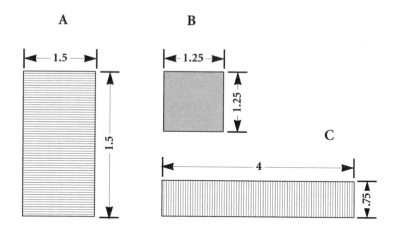

See answers on page 92.

Skateboard Contest

Five kids in the finals of the Fossil Street skateboard contest ride their boards from home to the site for the event. From the clues provided, figure out the kids' full names, the number of blocks each has to ride to the contest, and the street on which they live.

1. Chestnut Avenue is 4 blocks farther away than where Roger lives.
2. Ms. Mander lives on Main Street, 8 blocks away from Lenny.
3. Cooper lives 3 blocks from Linden and 7 blocks from Kenny.
4. Chapman lives six blocks farther away than 11th Street.
5. Kenny, whose last name starts with "L", lives closer than Sally.
6. Jimmy lives on Elm Street.

Blocks from Fossil St.

	Jimmy	Sally	Lenny	Roger	Kenny	1	3	7	8	11
Linden										
Lyle										
Mander										
Cooper										
Chapman										
Elm St.										
Main St.										
Chestnut Ave.										
Acorn Dr.										
11th St.										
1					
3					
7					
8					
11					

See answers on page 92.

59

Slug Crawl

Several prominent slugs entered the annual crawling contest recently. Last year's winner, Slippo, is favored to win again this year. A newcomer, Slig, is considered a "dark slug."

See if you can work out the clues and deduce each slug's crawl distance (in centimetres), the color of his leash, and the name of his owner.

1. The purple-leashed slug crawled 2.1.
2. Bob is not the owner of Oozey.
3. Slimeball wore green.
4. The slug who went .6 belongs to Bill.
5. Slig wore red.
6. The winner wore blue.
7. Woozey was not last.
8. Walter's slug did not wear green or blue.
9. Slimeball went half as far as Woozey.
10. Jack's slug was the winner.
11. Gooey crawled .2 less than Slippo.
12. The yellow-leashed slug crawled 1.8.
13. Gerald's slug, who crawled 1.5, wore red.
14. Harry owns Gooey.

See answers on page 93.

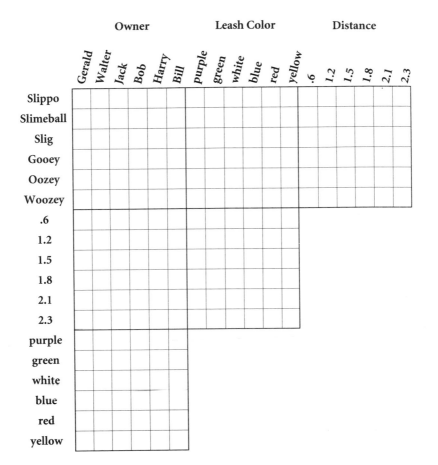

Square Count

In a checkerboard there are over 200 squares.

There are 32 squares that look like this: ☐

And 32 that look like this: ■

There are some that look like this:

And some like this:

Using the checkerboard shown below, see if you can find all the squares in each of the following rows and columns.

1. Columns A & B, rows 1–8
2. Columns A, B, & C, rows 1–3
3. Columns B, C, & D, rows 1–4
4. Columns A, B, C, & D, rows 2–4
5. Columns C, D, & E, rows 1–5
6. Columns A, B, & C, rows 1–6
7. Columns A–D, rows 1–4.

See answers on page 93.

Hint: It might help to mark off the sections as you count them.

62

Taber's Birdhouse

Taber, who is building a birdhouse, is making a scale drawing of the project. The chart below shows the areas (in centimetres) of each piece. See if you can match them with the pieces they represent.

1. The length of the side is 3.2 centimetres.
2. The width of the top is 1.25.
3. The narrowest piece is the back, with a width of just .8 centimetres.
4. The bottom is 2.75 centimetres long and 2.0 wide.
5. One piece is 2.5 by 1.6.
6. Two pieces have the same dimension: 2.0. The side is one of them.
7. The top looks like this:

	6.4	2.8	4.0	3.25	5.5
top					
side					
front					
bottom					
back					

See answers on page 93.

Time Zone

Nick, who lives in Boston, decided to phone seven of his friends for a conference call. It was 7:00 a.m. there when he began making the calls. Using the clues below, try to determine where the seven friends are located. (It might be a help to look at a globe or atlas.)

1. Lori was awakened by the phone ringing at 5:00 a.m.
2. Duke was having a noon meal.
3. Cary was 5 hours later than Deb.
4. Gene just finished lunch and was sitting down for a 1 o'clock meeting when the phone rang.
5. Jan was watching a late-night TV news show, which started at midnight.
6. Alex was 10 hours earlier than where Duke was.

	Boston, USA	London, England	Wellington, New Zealand	Honolulu, Hawaii	Nairobi, Kenya	Perth, Australia	Mazatlán, Mexico	Cape Town, South Africa
Nick	X							
Lori								
Deb								
Jan								
Duke								
Cary								
Alex								
Gene								

See answers on page 94.

Turkeys in the Road

Farmer McLynden just spilled crates of turkeys—all over Highway #246!

When those birds were on the truck they were in six crates, 50 to each crate, merrily on their way to market to meet the happy-turkey butcher. (Sshhh, turkeys don't know what a butcher is or they wouldn't be so happy!) But when that tire blew! Wow-e-e-e-ee! Now the turkeys are out of the crates and running all over the place, and farmer McLynden is having a hard time gathering them up and getting them back into the crates.

Finally, when all the chickens he can find are re-crated, McLynden's turkey-head count tells him that some of the gobblers got away (maybe they were helped, because we all know turkeys just aren't that smart). Anyway, there are no longer fifty birds in each of the crates.

Using the clues below, figure out how many turkeys are now in each of the six crates.

1. There are 233 turkeys left.
2. One end crate has the most turkeys in it; the other end has the fewest, a difference of 13 turkeys.
3. Crate #3 has 6 more turkeys than #2
4. Crate #5 has 2 fewer turkeys than #1.
5. Crate #4 has 35 turkeys, three more than the crate with the fewest.

Ye Olde Turkey Crates

| 1 | 2 | 3 | 4 | 5 | 6 |

See answers on page 94.

Vegetable Soup Contest

Five people each bought 15 cans of vegetables for a soup contest. No one bought the same number of any one kind, but 5 of one kind, 4 of another, 3 of another, and so on. Also, no vegetable was bought in the same quantity by any two people. Given all that, can you figure out how many cans of each vegetable each person bought and how much the purchases cost? Also, who won the contest for the tastiest soup?

1. The person who spent $6.43 bought 5 cans of asparagus and 3 cans of beans.
2. Lily spent the least amount of money, $1.66 less than T-bone. She bought 3 cans of carrots, 5 of peas, and 1 of corn.
3. Benny spent $1.20 on asparagus and $1.55 for corn and peas.
4. Joshua bought 2 cans of peas and spent $4.52 for his corn and carrots combined.
5. The person who won the contest bought 1 can of carrots and spent $7.42 total, 99¢ more than Benny.
6. T-bone spent the most. He bought 5 cans of corn, 4 of beans, and 1 of asparagus.

	corn	peas	carrots	asparagus	beans	amt. spent	winner
Benny							
Lily							
T-Bone							
Slim							
Joshua							

Shopping List	
corn	58¢
peas	39¢
carrots	44¢
asparagus	24¢
beans	64¢

See answers on page 94.

DIFFICULT PUZZLES

Boxes

The sixteen boxes below are each worth the number inside. Their names are intersections of rows (letters) and columns (numbers), i.e., the lower left corner box is D-1 or 1-D. It is worth 9 points.

	1	2	3	4
A	11	6	15	3
B	5	8	12	10
C	16	1	14	7
D	9	2	13	4

Four boys playing a game are trying to make the most points by trading boxes. Everyone must have four boxes at all times. From the clues, how many points does each boy have at game's end?

1. Jeremy didn't own any of the boxes in the A row.
2. Boyd's highest number is A-3.
3. B-2 and C-1 belong to the same boy, who isn't Bryce.
4. Bryce doesn't own any boxes in the 1 column.
5. On the last play of the game, Jeremy traded his 4-B for B-1.
6. D-2, A-2, and D-3 all belong to the same player.
7. C-1, B-3, and 4-D all belong to the same player.
8. Kevin's score was 4 higher than Boyd's.
9. Three of Boyd's boxes are in the A row.
10. Jeremy has just one box in the B row, which is B-1.

	1	2	3	4	5	6	7	8	9	10	11	12	13	14	15	16
Bryce																
Jeremy																
Boyd																
Kevin																

See answers on page 84.

Elevator

Ives and Newell are in charge of counting the people who get on and off the elevator in a hotel. They take turns riding to the top floor and back down, counting as they go. After two such trips each morning, two around noon, and two in the evening, there is an average taken.

The hotel manager wants to know today's average.

1. On Newell's noon trip there were 32 fewer people than in his morning count.
2. Ives counted a total of 122 in the morning and noon counts, just one higher than his evening count, but 24 more than Newell's evening count.
3. Ives's morning count is the same as Newell's average.
4. Ives's evening count was 37 more than Newell's morning count.

	morning	noon	evening	total	average
Ives					
Newell					

See answers on page 86.

Hint: Clue 2 gives most of the information needed to get started.

Figs

Brandon is a fig counter. The figs are kept in five boxes. Using the following clues, see if you can figure out how many figs are in the boxes today. (There are no fractions of figs; whole figs only!)

While you're at it, figure out the average number of figs in all five boxes.

1. The total number of figs in box C is ⅓ of half the total of those in box E.
2. Box B has twice as many figs as C and E combined.
3. There are 120 figs in one of the boxes.
4. Box A has half as many figs as E, which is also 10 fewer than D.
5. D has ¼ as many as B.

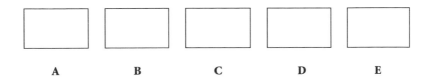

A   B   C   D   E

See answers on page 86.

Hint: The math for this puzzle is relatively easy. The key to solving it is to first identify the box that has 120 figs in it. It can only be done, however, through trial and error.

Foul Shots

Sometimes they make 'em, sometimes they don't! Using your excellent understanding of percentage, see if you can figure out the foul-shooting percentage for each of these six players this season. The highest is 83%. The lowest is 57%.

1. Player #34 had 102 successful shots, 30 fewer than the player who shot 71%.
2. The player with 57% (not #49 or #22) attempted 176 shots.
3. The player with 98 attempts shot 59%.
4. Player #27 shot 66%.
5. Player #12 had the fewest attempts and shot 80%.
6. The player with the highest percentage (not #18) made 38 fewer shots than #49.

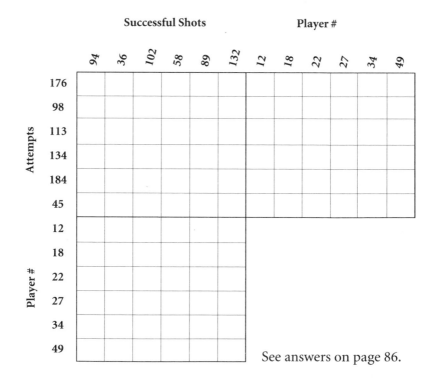

See answers on page 86.

Garage Sale

Ms. Gaskin found a clothing item. A man who had searched for years bought an old dresser. All were happy to have saved money. Who bought what? What were the original and purchase prices?

1. The bicycle was bought at 50% off. The buyer's name starts with H.
2. Ms. Cullen bought the item priced at $15.00 for ⅘ths that amount.
3. The tires sold for $1.00 less than the asking price.
4. The item that sold for $0.50 was an article of clothing.
5. Mr. Pazzini spent $4.00 less than Ms. Cullen.
6. Ms. Higgins paid for her dress with a $20.00 bill and received $19.25 in change.
7. Ms. Gaskin spent less for her item than Mr. Schmidt, who spent less than Mr. Pazzini.
8. The item originally priced the highest didn't sell for the highest price, nor did the lowest-priced item sell for the lowest amount.

	dress	sweater	dresser	telephone	tires	bicycle	$8	$6	$12	$10	75¢	50¢
Ms. Gaskin												
Mr. Pazzini												
Mr. Schmidt												
Ms. Cullen												
Ms. Higgins												
Mr. Havill												
$2						
$15						
$3						
$20						
$9						
$12						

Price Paid (column group header)

Original Price (row group header)

See answers on page 87.

Great Pencil Sale

Four sixth-grade classes decided to sell pencils to raise money to go to a concert. Each class bought 500 pencils for $0.03 each (this cost must be deducted before any profit is made). They agreed that the class that made the most money (each class was allowed to charge any amount for their pencils) could sit in the front row at the concert.

Using the clues below, figure out how much profit each class made, and which class got to sit in the front row.

1. The least amount of profit was $11.30 less than the winning amount.
2. Mr. Pendip's class made $3.80 more in profit than the class that sold its pencils at 10 for 75¢
3. The class that sold 219 pencils was not Mr. Pendip's.
4. Ms. Rimdrip's class sold its pencils for 7¢ more per pencil than Mr. Slimhip's class.

	219	375	413	500	5/40¢	10/75¢	10¢	15¢	$ profit	front row
Mr. Pendip										
Ms. Glenwhip										
Ms. Rimdrip										
Mr. Slimhip										

Number Sold — Selling Price

See answers on page 88.

Hint: Use trial and error to determine the answer to clue #2 (the difference between Pendip's profit and Glenwhip's). Remember to deduct the original cost of the pencils from the profits when it is calculated.

Hidden Grades

Ms. Stonebelt told four of her best math students that their grades were hidden in the charts below. Using all the clues, see if you can figure out the grade each one received.

1. Dan's percentage is B + K - ½C.
2. Bernard's grade is based on G + I + D - Dan's percentage plus sixty-five.
3. Jason earned a grade higher than Bernard. He scored 2E ÷ 3 + (½J) - 2.
4. Dexter's grade, the only one of the four without a plus or a minus, was derived from:
$$(A + C - [½F]) \times ⅕G ÷ 10 + ½J$$

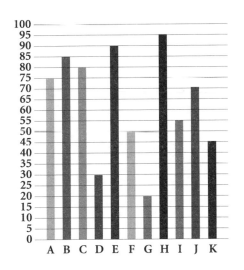

Grading System	
96–100	A
92–95	A–
89–91	B+
84–88	B
81–83	B–
77–80	C+
72–76	C
69–71	C–
62–68	D
0–61	F

See answers on page 88.

High Rent

A group of six people, who live in the same apartment building, got together one day for lunch. As they ate and talked, they discovered that each one lived on a different floor and that no one paid the same amount of rent. In fact, they learned that the higher the floor, the higher the rent, and that one person's rent is $525.

Your task is to figure out from the following clues the full names of the six renters, the floor on which each lives, and the amount of rent they pay.

1. Ms. Jordan lives between Danielle and Adams.
2. The highest rent is not paid by Falk, Stuart, or Peter. It is $175 more than the 17th floor.
3. Floor 21 is rented at $75 more than where Adams lives and $50 less than what Adrienne pays.
4. Sarah pays $475, $175 less than Ms. Drake.
5. Price's rent is $50 higher than Adrienne's and $100 more than Jacob's.
6. The rent at the 12th floor is $450. No one with the initial P or A lives there.
7. Stuart's rent is lower than Jordan's.

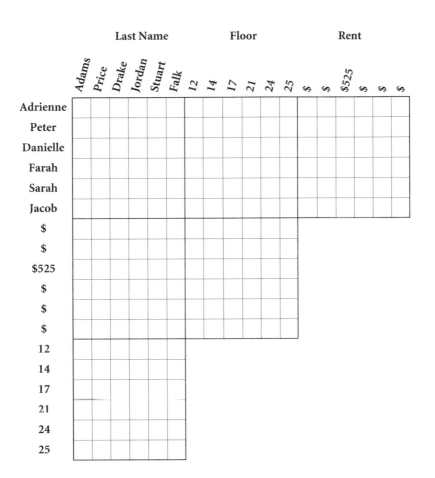

See answers on page 88.

Hundred-Miler

In a 100-mile bicycle race, Chet and his friends finished within 31 minutes of each other! From the clues, find each rider's last name, the bike color, the time each finished, and his average speed.

1. Both Dave and Seig rode over 6½ hours. Dave's bike is grey.
2. Day's bike, which beat Seig's green one, is blue.
3. The rider who rode for 6:32 hours was on a red bike.
4. Rick and the rider of the red bike both averaged under 16 mph.
5. The tan bike averaged 16.42.
6. The blue bike's rider is not Kurt, nor the one who took 6:40 hrs.
7. Brown, who rode in 6:09, is not Kurt or Bob.
8. Kurt's average beat Johns, who beat the green bike rider.

	Day	Johns	Seig	Brown	White	6:32	6:40	6:09	6:21	6:39	tan	grey	red	blue	green
Chet															
Dave															
Bob															
Kurt															
Rick															
15.65															
15.82															
15.62															
16.42															
16.10															
tan															
grey															
red															
blue															
green															

See answers on page 88.

Motorcycle

Old Mrs. Frizzle needed a new motorcycle because her old one was worn out from so many trips to town. She summoned her five sons—Luke, Jake, Swizzle, Jeremiah, and Malcolm—and told them, "Boys, I need a new motorcycle. It must be purple and it must have one extra tire. Also, I must have a new helmet, a new leather outfit, and new goggles. The one who finds me the best deal shall earn a handsome prize."

The sons met secretly and agreed that each would buy one of the five items and they would split the prize as follows: the one who bought the motorcycle would get 50% of the prize, the one who bought the tire would get 20%, the ones buying the outfit and the helmet would each get 12%, and the one buying the goggles would get 6%.

See if you can deduce which son bought which of the five items, and how much Mrs. Frizzle gave as a prize.

1. Swizzle Frizzle did not buy the helmet.
2. Malcolm earned 60¢ less than Jake.
3. Luke earned more than Jeremiah but less than Swizzle.
4. The one who bought the helmet—not Malcolm—earned 90¢.

	Motor-cycle	Tire	Helmet	Outfit	Goggles	Prize Money
Luke						
Jake						
Swizzle						
Jeremiah						
Malcolm						

See answers on page 89.

Hint: Start with clue #4, then go to clue #2.

Party Time

Aunt Hildy is having another wild tea party—on Sunday at 3 p.m. sharp! Aunt Hildy does not like guests to arrive early or late! (A nephew was cut out of her will for being seven seconds late to a dinner honoring her cat, Fred.) Now Aunt Hildy has put you in charge of making sure that everyone arrives *precisely* on time.

Since you know how far everyone lives from Aunt Hildy (the total mileage is 1131 miles for all five), you want to send letters to them specifying the average speed they must travel and the time they must leave in order to arrive exactly at 3:00 p.m. Using the clues, work out the correct information to send and keep handy.

1. Cousin Ansel will leave half an hour before Niece Gwendolyn.
2. Great Aunt Lucille will average 64 mph (no tickets, please!).
3. Nephew Fredrick needs to leave at 11:00 a.m.
4. Gwendolyn lives 319 miles away, 111 more than Great Aunt Lucille.
5. Ansel will travel a steady 58 miles per hour.
6. Uncle Jed lives 60 miles away and needs to leave at 1:30 p.m.
7. The one who leaves at 11:45 lives 12 miles farther than the one who lives 4 hours away.

	Miles from Aunt Hildy	Average Speed (mph)	Hours from Aunt Hildy	Departure Time
Great Aunt Lucille				
Nephew Fredrick				
Uncle Jed				
Niece Gwendolyn				
Cousin Ansel				

See answers on page 90.

Hints: The total mileage is the "key" needed to compute Ansel's distance from Aunt Hildy. Find miles per hour (mph) by dividing miles by hours. Or, determine mph and hours and compute the miles.

Roommates

Twelve people share six college rooms. Match each with their roommates, room numbers, and the color of their rooms.

1. Kris and Terry share a room.
2. Diane's roommate is not Sandra.
3. Duke does not live in #6, which is yellow.
4. Neither #5 or #4 is blue or beige.
5. The pink room has an odd number, but it not #3.
6. April lives in #5 with Sandra.
7. Dawn's roommate is not Tina.
8. The blue room is even numbered.
9. Jason lives in the green room; Sandra in the white one.
10. Sue is not in #3.
11. Gary's room is blue.

	Sandra	Tina	Duke	Jason	Sue	Kris	blue	green	yellow	beige	pink	white	1	2	3	4	5	6
Greg																		
Dawn																		
Terry																		
April																		
Diane																		
Gary																		
1																		
2																		
3																		
4																		
5																		
6																		
blue													
green													
yellow													
beige													
pink													
white													

Room No.

See answers on pages 91–92.

Hint: Strangely, the girls' rooms are odd numbered and the boys have even-numbered rooms.

Runners

After these eight runners finished practice, they compared how far each had run and how many minutes it had taken them. Using the clues given below, determine how many kilometres each of the runners ran and their average speed per kilometre. (We've provided a simple chart for converting miles to kilometres. It's sure to be a help, unless you're already a computer brain!)

1. Darlene spent 99 minutes running 1.86 miles farther than Kerry.
2. Todd ran 3.72 miles fewer than Wendy.
3. Peter, who ran 3.1 miles in 35 minutes, ran farther than Bob, who ran for 30 minutes.
4. Wendy's total time was 3 hours, 18 minutes.
5. Sandy ran .62 miles farther than Lynn.
6. Lynn ran an average of 2 minutes per kilometre slower than Sandy.
7. For one runner, the average minutes per kilometre and the number of kilometres run were the same number.

Conversion Chart	
miles	kilometres
.62	1
1.24	2
1.86	3
2.48	4
3.10	5
3.72	6
4.34	7
4.96	8
5.58	9
6.20	10

	Sandy	Peter	Wendy	Kerry	Todd	Bob	Darlene	Lynn
18								
12								
11								
10								
9								
8								
5								
4								
7.0								
7.5								
8.0								
8.5								
9.0								
9.5								
10.5								
11.0								

Kilometres

Minutes

See answers on page 92.

Stephanie's Investments

Stephanie invested some of her money into five companies. She recently received information regarding how much money she made or lost on each. Using the clues below, figure out what product each company sold, how much Stephanie invested in each, and her loss or profit.

1. Dowin Products showed a 30% profit. Stephanie's profit for that product was $30.
2. Stephanie made the most money from the paint company, which was not Corbett or Cortell.
3. Aluminum was Stephanie's worst investment, costing her $160.
4. Alaco makes siding. Cortell does not produce soft drinks.
5. Corbett & Sons showed a 20% loss.
6. Stephanie invested $300 into Cortell.
7. Her $200 investment cost her 5%.
8. Smith and Co. returned $50 to Stephanie.

	paper products	aluminum	soft drinks	paint	siding	10% profit	20% loss	30% profit	5% loss	15% profit
Smith and Co.										
Alaco										
Dowin Products										
Corbett & Sons										
Cortell										
Investment $200										
$100										
$500										
$300										
$800										

See answers on page 93.

Tallest

Six friends decided to turn out for basketball. One of the things their coach did first was to measure their heights. Using the clues, and the shapes with numbers (in inches) below, figure out how tall each boy is.

S = the sum of the numbers inside the square
C = the sum of the numbers inside the circle
T = the sum of the numbers inside the triangle
R = the sum of the numbers inside the rectangle

1. Brad's height is 2T − 15.
2. Kevin's height is T ÷ by the only number found in all four shapes, times ten, + 3.
3. Monte's height is S − R, times the only number in just the triangle and the rectangle, minus the only number in just the square and the rectangle.
4. Duane's height is C ÷ 4, plus 3, times 3.
5. Kris's height is T + C, divided by the next to the lowest number in the circle, times the next to the lowest number in the rectangle, minus seven.
6. Tom's height is S − 1 ÷ by the largest number in the triangle, times the largest number in the square, minus the three numbers that lie in the circle only, plus seven.

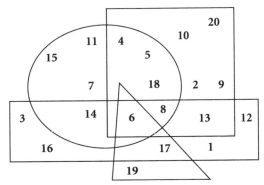

See answers on page 93.

SOLUTIONS

Auction

Irene Black bought cheese ($5). Denise Green bought pie ($4). Duane Grey bought coffee ($7). Dan White bought cake ($6). Elroy Brown bought fruit ($3.50).

Biology Class

Kate adopted Willy, the mole (18 cm). Kristen adopted Weldon, the ladybug (1.3 cm). Kurt adopted Walter, the fly (1 cm). Kristi adopted Wendy, the rat (14 cm). Kyle adopted Warren, the bat (11 cm). Kevin adopted Wanda, the hamster (23 cm).

Boxes

Bryce had 2, 6, 10, and 13 for 31 total.
Jeremy had 1, 5, 9, and 14 for 29 total.
Boyd had 3, 7, 11, and 15 for 36 total.
Kevin had 4, 8, 12, and 16 for 40 total.

Caleb's Checkbook

Caleb Jones started with $1987 but now has $681.
Barbara Jackson started with $1749 but now has $423.
Sam Brown started with $1699 but now has $1004.
Joyce Wilson started with $1940 but now has $970.
Millard Smith started with $2050 but is now overdrawn $45!

Chicken Mountain

Chicken-grading formula results: Saffola 242.5; McSanders 257.6 (winner); McPlume 172.2; McCombe 224.9; Poularde 196.6.

Chocolate Chip Cookies

Ms. Effie Bundt puts in 5 chips and bakes for 16 min 17 sec.
Ms. Ruby Strudel puts in 7 chips and bakes for 17 min 7 sec.
Ms. Thelma Spicer puts in 8 chips and bakes for 16 min 9 sec.
Ms. Miriam Applestreet puts in 9 chips and bakes for 17 min.
Ms. Georgia Honeydew puts in 10 chips, baking for 17 min 8 sec.

Coast to Coast

The route that Jacques and Chi Chi travelled took them in order to: Phoenix, Los Angeles, San Francisco, Portland, Salt Lake City, Denver, Dallas, St. Louis, Chicago, Pittsburgh, and finally to Washington, D.C.

Coffee

Max drinks 4 cups, with 2 sugars, no milk.
Doris drinks 5 cups, with 1 sugar, milk.
Blizzo drinks 1 cup, with no sugar, no milk.
Jan drinks 6 cups, with 6 sugars, milk.
Boris drinks 8 cups, with 4 sugars, no milk.

Decimal Ruler

The lengths of the lines are: **a** 3.3; **b** 1.3; **c** 3.9; **d** 2.8; **e** 0.6; **f** 3.8; **g** 1.8.

Dessert

Jane Brown ate ⅔ of the custard.
Pete Smith ate ⅙ of the apple pie.
Tom Grey ate ¾ of the fig cookie.
Sarah Jones ate ⅛ of the chocolate cake.

Destry's Missing Numbers

The squares are: **A** 22.34; **B** 11.93; **C** 25.17; **D** 13.47; **E** 25.71.

Dog Apartments

Name	Apt. No.	Food/Week	Baths/Month
MacTavish	408	2 lbs.	9
Chico	103	10 lbs.	3
Ivan	609	8 lbs.	12
Wilfred	512	4 lbs.	2
Taz	221	12 lbs.	6
Spunky	341	6 lbs.	4

E.F. Bingo

Wanda won when the ¹⁶/₁₈ths fraction was called.

Elevator

	Morning	Noon	Evening	Total	Average
Ives	78	44	121	243	81
Newell	84	52	98	234	78

Famous Person

J O H N F K E N N E D Y

Field Trip

Jorn weighs 45.1 qinae, or 4.1 Earth ounces (Eo), Duloc weighs 42.9 qinae (3.9 Eo), Phren weighs 63.8 qinae (5.8 Eo), Sio weighs 50.6 qinae (4.6 Eo), and Ontrus weighs 15.4 qinae (1.4 Eo).

Figs

The number of figs in the five boxes are: **A** 60; **B** 280; **C** 20; **D** 70; **E** 120.

Fishing

Fred, using worms, caught one fish. Sammy, using dry flies, caught three fish. Torkel, using eggs, caught two fish. Joe, using flatfish, caught no fish at all.

Flea Market Leftovers

Dan took the nut. Sandy took the bolt. Bob took the pencil. Irene took the pencil sharpener. Doris took the compass.

Flighty Decimals

In the square:	4.39	4.01	2.60	1.42	total: 12.42
In the circle:	5.20	1.16	.07	.03	total: 6.46
In the rectangle:	3.71	1.01	.72	.30	total: 5.74

Foul Shots

Player #12 made 36 foul shots out of 45 attempts, for 80%.
Player #18 made 58 foul shots out of 98 attempts, for 59%.
Player #22 made 94 foul shots out of 113 attempts, for 83%.
Player #27 made 89 foul shots out of 134 attempts, for 66%.
Player #34 made 102 foul shots out of 176 attempts, for 57%.
Player #49 made 132 foul shots out of 184 attempts, for 71%.

Four Cups

Cup **A** has 8 oz. of apple juice, **B** has 3 oz. of water, **C** has 11 oz. of oil, and **D** has 5 oz. of vinegar.

Fractions Prom

Table 1:	⅓	⅔	⅙	⅚
Table 2:	¼	⅛	⅜	⅞
Table 3:	⅕	¹⁄₁₀	⅖	⅗

Fund-Raiser

Tinzen won the CD player; and room 125 won the field trip to the amusement park.

Garage Sale

Ms. McGaskin bought the sweater for $0.50; original price $3.
Mr. Pazzini bought the tires for $8.00; originally $9.
Mr. Schmidt bought the dresser for $6; originally $12.
Ms. Cullen bought the telephone for $12; originally $15.
Ms. Higgins bought the dress for $0.75; originally $2.
Mr. Havill bought the bicycle for $10; originally $20.

Golf

Player	1	2	3	4	5	6	7	8	9	Total
Jim	5	5	4	4	6	6	5	3	4	42
Jan	4	7	3	4	5	5	5	4	3	40
Jon	6	5	4	5	5	6	4	5	3	43
Jed	5	6	3	4	5	6	5	6	4	44

Jed was the lazy scorekeeper.

Grade Book

Student	Score Missed	Total	Average	Grade
Alban	18	495	55	C
Astrid	62	495	55	C
Amos	48	549	61	B
Angus	68	558	62	A
Avril	33	531	59	B

Great Pencil Sale

Mr. Pendip sold 413 at 10¢ each for a $26.30 profit (front row seats).
Ms. Glenwhip sold 500 at 10 for 75¢, for a profit of $22.50.
Ms. Rimdrip sold 219 at 15¢ each, for a profit of $17.85.
Mr. Slimhip sold 375 at 5 for 40¢ for a profit of $15.00.

Heather's Garden

Heather has: 3 rows of carrots, 4 rows of cabbages, 1 row of turnips, 2 rows of pole beans, 5 rows of spinach, and 6 rows of cucumbers.

Hidden Grades

Dan scored 90 (B+); Bernard got 80 (C+); Jason got the highest grade, 93 (A−); Dexter got 87 (B).

High Rent

Adrienne Drake lives on 24 and pays $650.
Peter Adams lives on 17 and pays $525.
Danielle Stuart lives on 12 and pays $450.
Farah Price lives on 25 and pays $700.
Sarah Jordan lives on 14 and pays $475.
Jacob Falk lives on 21 and pays $600.

Hot Dogs

Gerald Jones, in room 205, ate 20 hot dogs.
Isabella Smith, in room 202, ate 12 hot dogs.
Germaine Brown, in room 201, ate 24 hot dogs.
Tony Green, in room 204, ate 16 hot dogs.
Ginger White, in room 203, ate 22 hot dogs.

Hundred Miler

Chet Brown rode the tan bike in 6:09 hours to average 16.42.
Dave Johns rode the grey bike in 6:39 hours to average 15.65.
Bob Day rode the blue bike in 6:21 hours to average 16.10.
Kurt White rode the red bike in 6:32 hours to average 15.82.
Rick Seig rode the green bike in 6:40 hours to average 15.62.

Jump Rope

Danielle made 12 jumps; Gary made 9 jumps; Jan jumped 20 times;

Arnie jumped 17 times; and Ruth made 25 jumps before missing a jump.

Longest Drive

Desmond Rivers drove 257m/236yds with a 3-wood.
Simon Bates drove 263m/242yds with a 2-iron.
Lyle Reed drove 244m/224yds with a 5-wood.
Lester Baring drove 283m/260yds with a driver.
Henry Jenkins drove 282m/259yds with a 3-wood.
Jake Pym drove 261m/240yds with a driver.

Lunch at Paul's

Paul brought the olives and bought the coffee for $2.75.
Julie brought the cake and bought the cheese for $2.70.
Sandra brought the pickles and bought the mayonnaise for $2.18.
Diane brought the fruit and bought the chicken for $4.80.
Wally brought the salad and bought the bread for $4.17.

Mathathon

The girls defeated the boys 80 to -10.

Motorcycle

Luke bought the helmet and got 90¢. Jake bought the tire and got $1.50. Swizzle bought the motorcycle and earned $3.75. Jeremiah bought the goggles and earned 45¢. Malcolm bought the outfit and got 90¢. The "handsome prize" was $7.50.

Notes: The puzzle "key" is the prize money promised by old Mrs. Frizzle. Knowing from clue #4 that 90¢ represents 12%, you divide $.90 by .12 to get $7.50, the "handsome prize." Then, you can determine that 50% of $7.50 is $3.75, that 20% is $1.50, and that 6% is 45¢. From clue #2, you know that Malcolm can have only 90¢, because any other amount plus 60¢ would not total any of the other amounts. Therefore, Jake has $1.50, meaning he bought the tire.

Mountain Climb

Dacon climbed Mirre (7500-foot elevation). Drakon climbed Old Baldy (4500). Macom climbed Goat (8000). Bacon climbed Sleepy (9000). Jake climbed Raleigh (11,000).

Mountain Race

Andy Stiller climbs Mt. Stewart carrying 20 lbs.
Gerald Brown climbs Mt. Morgan carrying 40 lbs.
Dale Dorsey climbs Mt. Waring carrying 50 lbs.
Paul Anderson climbs Mt. McIntire carrying 30 lbs.
Jim McGee climbs Mt. Picard carrying 10 lbs.

Multiplication Jeopardy

Sue Jensen	8×15	=	120
June James	9×16	=	144
Dale Johnson	5×14	=	70
Neil Johns	7×18	=	126
Tina Jones	11×13	=	143

Ned's Newspaper Route

The Joneses live in the green house and get a *daily only* (clue #4).
The Johnsons live in the blue house and get a Sunday only
The Smiths live in the grey house and get a Sunday only.
The Browns live in the white house and get both daily and Sunday.
The Simpsons live in the yellow house and also get both papers.

Old House

The Barneses lived 11 years in the red-painted house.
The Carpenters lived 44 years in the green-painted house.
The Lewises lived 5 years in the blue-painted house.
The Parkers lived 2 years in the yellow-painted house.
The Smiths lived 22 years in the brown-painted house.
The Warners lived 4 years in the white-painted house.

Party Time

Guest	Distance in Miles	Average mph	Hours Away	Departure Time
Great Aunt Lucille	208	64	3¼	11:45 a.m.
Nephew Fredrick	196	49	4	11:00 a.m.
Uncle Jed	60	40	1½	1:30 p.m.
Niece Gwendolyn	319	58	5½	9:30 a.m.
Cousin Ansel	348	58	6	9:00 a.m.

Play Ball

Teddie has a white soccer ball that weighs 16 oz.
Teresa has a orange golf ball that weighs 1.5 oz.
Toddy has a yellow Ping-Pong ball that weighs .8 oz.
Tanya has a green tennis ball that weighs 2 oz.
Tom has a brown basketball that weighs 22 oz.
Tillie has a red football that weighs 15 oz.

Pocket Change

Alex started with $4 and ended with 40¢. Scott started with $3 and ended with 95¢. Dan started with $2 and ended with 10¢. Jim started with $1 and ended with 70¢. Duane started with $2 and ended with $1.65.

Potato Chips

Elmo Glitzwhizzle ate 18 bags. Gazelda Kettledrummel ate 6 bags. Amos Grugenminer ate 12 bags. Gerald Crackenberry ate 9 bags. Sally Witteyspooner ate 3 bags. Hubert Jones ate 24 bags!

Queen Rachel's Bridge Toll

Chiquita wears black shoes and pays 18¢ bridge toll.
Cindy wears blue shoes and pays 36¢ bridge toll.
Kurt wears red shoes and pays 14¢ bridge toll.
Taber wears white shoes and pays 38¢ bridge toll.
Caleb wears green shoes and pays 24¢ bridge toll.

Rhoda Tiller

Figure	Name	Inside Angle	Outside Angle
A	Rhoda Tiller	17	163
B	Ed Able	58	122
C	Val Veda	75	105
D	Asper Gus	85	95
E	Ruta Baggy	61	119

Roommates

Greg and Jason live in green #4.
Dawn and Sue live in pink #1.
Terry and Kris live in yellow #6.

April and Sandra live in white #5.
Diane and Tina live in beige #3.
Gary and Duke live in blue #2.

Runners

Runner	Distance (km)	Average Time (min)
Sandy	10	8.5
Peter	5	7.0
Wendy	18	11.0
Kerry	8	8.0
Todd	12	9.5
Bob	4	7.5
Darlene	11	9.0
Lynn	9	10.5

Sand

Mr. Logan took 21.875%, or 26.25 lbs.
Mr. Driver took 3.125%, 3.75 lbs.
Mr. Thomas took 6.25%, 7.5 lbs.
Mr. Lang took 37.5%, 45 lbs.
Mr. Antonelli took 12.5%, 15 lbs.
Mr. Waters took 18.75%, 22.5 lbs.

Shapes

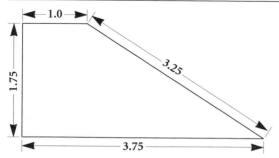

Skateboard Contest

Jimmy Cooper rode 8 blocks, from Elm St. Sally Mander rode 3, from Main St. Lenny Linden rode 11, from Chestnut Ave. Roger Chapman rode 7, from Acorn Dr. Kenny Lyle rode 1, from 11th St.

Slug Crawl

Gerald's Slig, who wears a red leash, crawled 1.5 cm.

Walter's Oozey, who wears a yellow leash, crawled 1.8 cm.

Jack's Slippo, who wears a blue leash, crawled 2.3 cm.

Bob's Woozey, who wears a white leash, crawled 1.2 cm.

Harry's Gooey, who wears a purple leash, crawled 2.1 cm.

Bill's Slimeball, who wears a green leash, crawled .6 cm.

Square Count

The number of squares in the sections are: **1.** 23; **2.** 14; **3.** 20; **4.** 20; **5.** 26; **6.** 32; **7.** 30.

Stephanie's Investments

Smith and Co. sold paint. Stephanie's profit on $500 was $50.

Alaco sold siding, and Stephanie lost $10 on her $200 investment.

Dowin Products sold soft drinks. Stephanie's profit on the $100 she invested was $30.

Corbett & Sons Co. sold aluminum. Stephanie lost $160 on her $800 investment in that company.

Cortell Co. sold paper products and made Stephanie a $45 profit on her investment of $300.

Sadly, the outcome of all Stephanie's various investments was a total loss of $45.

Taber's Birdhouse

The measurements in centimetres are: the top is 3.25, the side is 6.4, the front is 4.0, the bottom is 5.5, and the back is 2.8.

Tallest

The heights of the six friends are: Duane tallest at 75 inches; Tom 2nd at 74 in.; Kevin 3rd at 73 in.; Monte 4th at 72 in.; Kris 5th at 71 in.; Brad shortest at 69 in.

Temperature

The lowest temperature is at the 10:30 a.m. reading. The drop in temperature then is due to all the open doors as the students take their morning break.

Time Zone

Nick, as you know, is in Boston. Lori is in Mazatlán. Deb is in Nairobi. Jan is in Wellington. Duke is in London. Cary is in Perth. Alex is in Honolulu. Gene is in Cape Town.

Turkeys in the Road

Crate **1**: 45; **2**: 36; **3**: 42; **4**: 35, **5**: 43; and **6**: 32.

Vegetable Soup Contest

	Corn	Peas	Carrots	Asparagus	Beans	Spent
Benny	2	1	4	5	3	$6.43
Lily	1	5	3	4	2	$6.09
T-Bone	5	3	2	1	4	$7.75
Slim	3	4	1	2	5	$7.42 (winner)
Joshua	4	2	5	3	1	$6.66

Wild Numbers

¼	½	¾	1
$4/16$	.5	$6/8$	$5/5$
one-fourth	50%	.75	100%
$3/12$	$4/8$	three-fourths	$1.00
.250	half a dollar	$9/12$	whole
$6/24$	$7/14$	75%	$10/10$
$5/20$	$3/6$	75¢	$4/4$

Zox

Of 750 Zoxians, the island of Zog has 75 residents, Zod has 250, Zob has 150, Zop has 175, and Zoz has 100.

INFORMATIONAL CHART AND INDEX

Title	Pages Puz./Sol.	Skill	Difficulty	Grade	Solve Time
Auction	22/84	fractions	medium	5+	20–30
Biology Class	24/84	add/subtract	medium	4+	20–30
Boxes	67/84	coordinates	difficult	4+	30–40
Caleb's Checkbook	26/84	computation	medium	5+	30–40
Chicken Mountain	28/84	decimals	medium	6+	20–30
Chocolate Chip Cookies	30/84	measurement	medium	6+	20–30
Coast to Coast	8/85	coordinates	easy	4+	10–20
Coffee	9/85	multiplication	easy	4+	20–30
Decimal Ruler	10/85	measurement	easy	4+	15–20
Dessert	32/85	fractions	medium	5+	20–30
Destry's Missing Numbers	11/85	decimals	easy	6+	10–20
Dog Apartments	34/85	multiplication	medium	5+	20–30
E.F. Bingo	12/85	equiv. fractions	easy	5+	10–20
Elevator	68/86	averages	difficult	6+	30–40
Famous Person	13/86	pre-algebra	easy	5+	10–15
Field Trip	36/86	decimals	medium	6+	20–30
Figs	69/86	fractions	difficult	5+	30–40
Fishing	4/86	deductive reasoning	beginning	4+	10–15
Flea Market Leftovers	37/86	measurement	medium	5+	20–30
Flighty Decimals	14/86	decimals	easy	4+	10–20
Foul Shots	70/86	fractions	difficult	6+	40–50
Four Cups	38/87	measurement	medium	5+	20–30
Fractions Prom	39/87	fractions	medium	4+	20–30
Fund-Raiser	40/87	add/subtract	medium	4+	20–30
Garage Sale	71/87	deductive reasoning	difficult	5+	30–40
Golf	42/87	deductive reasoning	medium	6+	20–30
Grade Book	43/87	averages	medium	5+	20–30
Great Pencil Sale	72/88	computation	difficult	6+	40–50
Heather's Garden	15/88	add/subtract	easy	3+	20–30
Hidden Grades	73/88	graphs	difficult	6+	40–50
High Rent	74/88	deductive reasoning	difficult	6+	40–50
Hot Dogs	44/88	computation	medium	4+	20–30
Hundred-Miler	76/88	averages	difficult	6+	40–50
Jump Rope	5/88	computation	beginning	3+	20–30
Longest Drive	46/88	measurement	medium	6+	20–30
Lunch at Paul's	48/89	computation	medium	5+	20–30
Mathathon	16/89	decimals	easy	5+	20–30
Motorcycle	77/89	percent	difficult	6+	40–50

Title	Pages Puz./Sol.	Skill	Difficulty	Grade	Minutes
Mountain Climb	17/89	computation	easy	5+	20–30
Mountain Race	18/90	add/subtract	easy	4+	20–30
Multiplication Jeopardy	50/90	computation	medium	5+	20–30
Ned's Newspaper Route	19/90	deductive reasoning	easy	4+	20–30
Old House	51/90	add/subtract	medium	4+	20–30
Party Time	78/90	time/speed	difficult	6+	40–50
Play Ball	52/91	decimals	medium	6+	20–30
Pocket Change	6/91	add/subtract	beginning	4+	20–30
Potato Chips	54/91	computation	medium	6+	20–30
Queen Rachel's Bridge Toll	55/91	decimals	medium	6+	20–30
Rhoda Tiller	56/91	protractors	medium	6+	20–30
Roommates	79/91	deductive reasoning	difficult	6+	40–50
Runners	80/92	metrics	difficult	6+	40–50
Sand	57/92	decimals	medium	5+	20–30
Shapes	58/92	decimals	medium	4+	20–30
Skateboard Contest	59/92	add/subtract	medium	5+	20–30
Slug Crawl	60/93	decimals	medium	5+	20–30
Square Count	62/93	pre-geometry	medium	6+	20–30
Stephanie's Investments	82/93	percent	difficult	6+	40–60
Taber's Birdhouse	63/93	area in cm.	medium	6+	20–30
Tallest	83/93	pre-geometry	difficult	4+	20–30
Temperature	7/93	estimating	beginning	4+	15–20
Time Zone	64/94	time zones	medium	5+	20–30
Turkeys in the Road	65/94	deductive reasoning	medium	4+	20–30
Vegetable Soup Contest	66/94	computation	medium	5+	20–30
Wild Numbers	20/94	fractions	easy	5+	20–30
Zox	21/94	fractions	easy	5+	20–30